ISAAC ASIMOV'S NEW LIBRARY OF THE UNIVERSE

A DISTANT GIANT:
THE PLANET NEPTUNE

BY ISAAC ASIMOV
WITH REVISIONS AND UPDATING BY FRANCIS REDDY

Gareth Stevens Publishing
MILWAUKEE

For a free color catalog describing Gareth Stevens' list of high-quality books, call 1-800-542-2595 (USA) or 1-800-461-9120 (Canada). Gareth Stevens' Fax: (414) 225-0377.

The publisher gratefully acknowledges the generous assistance of Jurie van der Woude and the staff of Jet Propulsion Laboratory.

Library of Congress Cataloging-in-Publication Data

Asimov, Isaac.
  A distant giant: the planet Neptune / by Isaac Asimov; with
revisions and updating by Francis Reddy.
    p. cm. — (Isaac Asimov's New library of the universe)
  Rev. ed. of: Neptune: the farthest giant. 1990.
  Includes index.
  Summary: Describes the characteristics and movements of the planet
Neptune and how we found out about it.
  ISBN 0-8368-1231-X
  1. Neptune (Planet)—Juvenile literature. [1. Neptune (Planet)]
I. Asimov, Isaac. Neptune: the farthest giant. II. Title. III. Series:
Asimov, Isaac. New library of the universe.
QB691.A83 1996
523.4'81—dc20   95-40349

This edition first published in 1996 by
Gareth Stevens Publishing
1555 North RiverCenter Drive, Suite 201
Milwaukee, Wisconsin 53212, USA

Project editor: Barbara J. Behm
Design adaptation: Helene Feider
Editorial assistant: Diane Laska
Production director: Teresa Mahsem
Picture research: Matthew Groshek and Diane Laska

Printed in the United States of America

1 2 3 4 5 6 7 8 9 99 98 97 96

To bring this classic of young people's information up to date, the editors at Gareth Stevens Publishing have selected two noted science authors, Greg Walz-Chojnacki and Francis Reddy. Walz-Chojnacki and Reddy coauthored the recent book *Celestial Delights: The Best Astronomical Events Through 2001.*

Walz-Chojnacki is also the author of the book *Comet: The Story Behind Halley's Comet* and various articles about the space program. He was an editor of *Odyssey,* an astronomy and space technology magazine for young people, for eleven years.

Reddy is the author of nine books, including *Halley's Comet, Children's Atlas of the Universe, Children's Atlas of Earth Through Time,* and *Children's Atlas of Native Americans,* plus numerous articles. He was an editor of *Astronomy* magazine for several years.

CONTENTS

We live in an enormously large place – the Universe. It's just in the last fifty-five years or so that we've found out how large it probably is. It's only natural that we would want to understand the place in which we live, so scientists have developed instruments – such as radio telescopes, satellites, probes, and many more – that have told us far more about the Universe than could possibly be imagined.

We have seen planets up close. We have learned about quasars and pulsars, black holes, and supernovas. We have gathered amazing data about how the Universe may have come into being and how it may end. Nothing could be more astonishing.

In 1989, a probe called *Voyager 2* completed a twelve-year journey to the outer planets. It passed close to Neptune and its largest satellite, Triton. *Voyager 2* sent back to Earth bountiful information about these far-off worlds, particularly giant Neptune.

Isaac Asimov

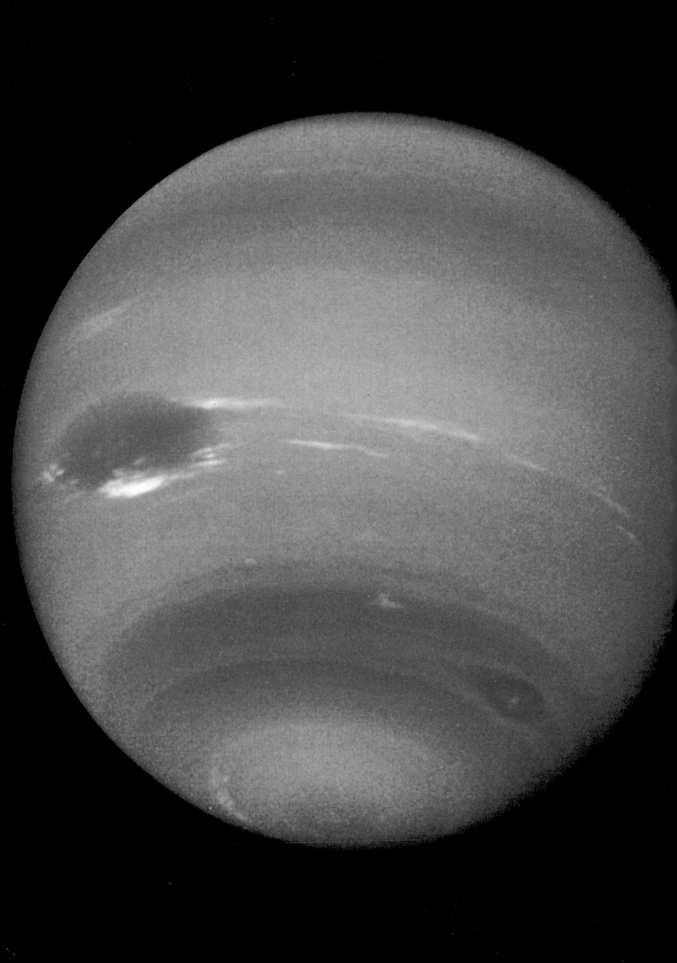

Neptune's Discovery

By the 1840s, it was clear that the motion of the most distant planet then known, Uranus, was not what scientists would consider normal.

Two researchers worked separately trying to explain this observation of Uranus. The men were John Couch Adams of England and Urbain Jean Joseph Leverrier of France. Each of them felt there must be a planet beyond Uranus that pulled at it and affected its motion. Each astronomer calculated where this planet might be.

Then in 1846, two German astronomers, Johann Gottfried Galle and Heinrich Ludwig d'Arrest, observed the sky in the area of Leverrier's calculations – and they found a new planet!

The bluish green planet was named *Neptune* after the Roman god of the sea. All four men – Galle, d'Arrest, Adams, and Leverrier – share credit in the discovery of Neptune.

Opposite: The blue face of Neptune, the last of the so-called giant planets. Bright cirrus clouds constantly surround the dark oval of an Earth-sized storm in Neptune's atmosphere.

Top: French mathematician Urbain Jean Joseph Leverrier.

Bottom: British astronomer John Couch Adams.

One of the Giants

There are four giant planets – Jupiter, Saturn, Uranus, and Neptune. Neptune is the most distant from Earth and the smallest of them. But it is still vast at about 30,450 miles (49,000 kilometers) across – four times wider than Earth. It is about 2.8 billion miles (4.5 billion km) from the Sun, thirty times farther from the Sun than Earth.

From Neptune, the Sun looks like a very bright star. Neptune gets only 1/900 of the light and warmth that Earth receives. Even so, sunshine on Neptune is 450 times brighter than light reflected to Earth from a full Moon.

Neptune orbits the Sun in 165 Earth years. A "day" on Neptune is about eighteen hours long.

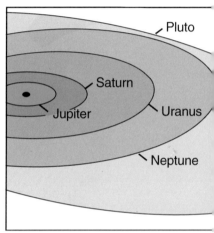

Opposite: A false-color picture of Neptune. Different colors represent different heights in Neptune's atmosphere. The lowest clouds are shaded dark blue; the highest clouds are pink. *Inset, top:* The orbits of the five outermost planets of our Solar System. Within Jupiter's orbit are the orbits of Mars, Earth, Venus, and Mercury. *Inset, bottom:* Unlike Earth *(pictured)*, one of the Solar System's "rocky" planets, Neptune is a giant ball of gases. It has no solid surface.

❓ *Which planet is the fastest of them all?*

Earth travels around the Sun at 18.6 miles (29.9 km) per second. That's much faster than even our fastest rockets travel. But the farther a planet is from the Sun, the weaker the Sun's gravitational pull on it and the slower the planet moves. Neptune is so distant from the Sun that it moves along its orbit at a speed of only 3.3 miles (5.3 km) per second. Mercury, the planet nearest the Sun, speeds along at nearly 30 miles (48 km) per second.

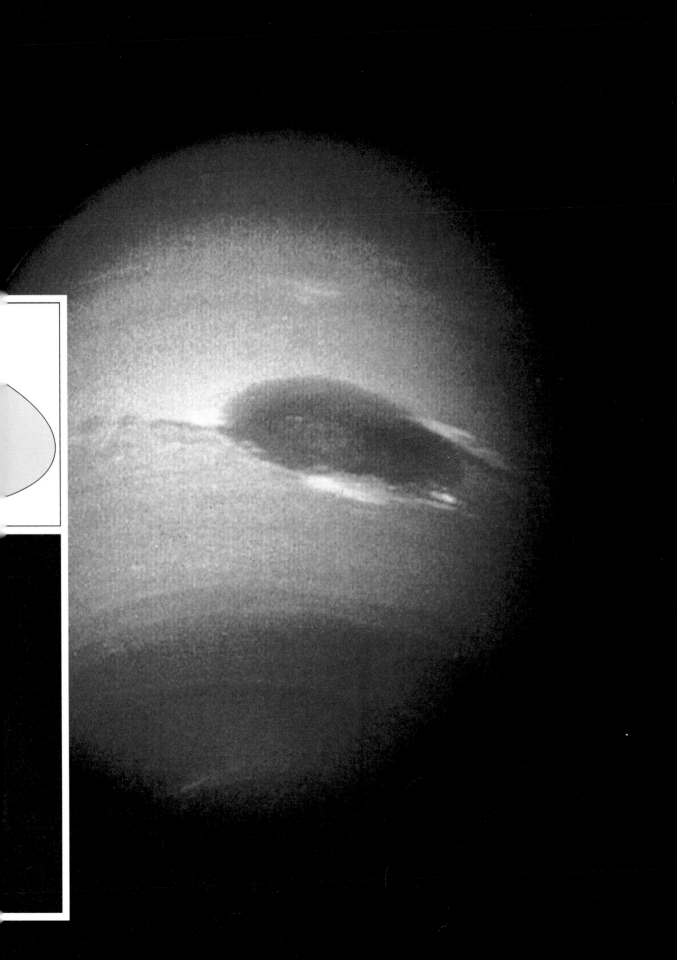

Triton and Nereid

Soon after Neptune was discovered, astronomers found a satellite circling it. This satellite, or moon, was named *Triton*, after the son of Poseidon, the sea god of ancient Greek myths.

Triton is a large satellite with a diameter of 1,700 miles (2,740 km), about 78 percent the diameter of Earth's Moon. It is about the same distance from Neptune as Earth's Moon is from Earth. Triton circles Neptune in just under six days. Earth's Moon circles Earth in about 27 1/3 days. Neptune is much larger than Earth. As a result, Triton's orbit takes less time because Neptune has a stronger gravitational pull than Earth.

In 1949, a second moon, Nereid, was discovered. It is about 210 miles (340 km) across and is much farther from Neptune than Triton – over fifteen times as far. It takes Nereid 360 days to orbit Neptune. This is about as long as it takes Earth to orbit the Sun.

Opposite: This photograph of Triton's speckled surface was taken by *Voyager 2. Inset:* Triton *(top arrow)* and Nereid *(bottom arrow)* are moons in orbit around Neptune.

Right: Nereid orbits Neptune in a wide, oval-shaped orbit. Triton is unlike most of the Solar System's moons in two ways – it orbits Neptune east to west, and its orbit is tilted at an angle to the planet's equator. The straight line shows the direction of Neptune's path around the Sun.

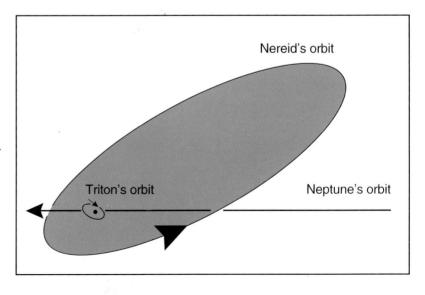

Nereid's orbit

Triton's orbit

Neptune's orbit

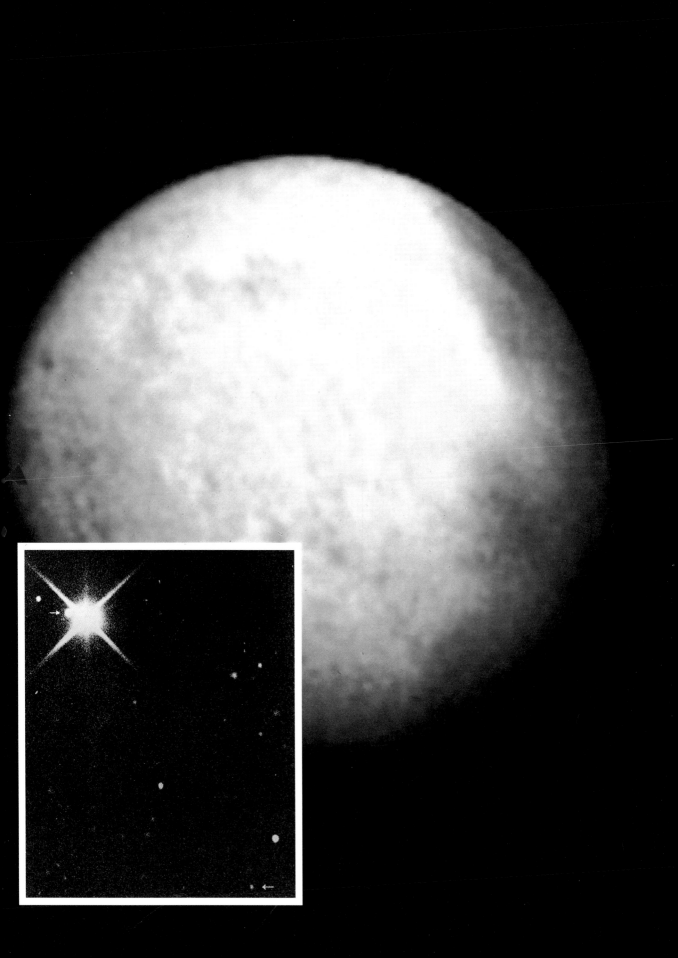

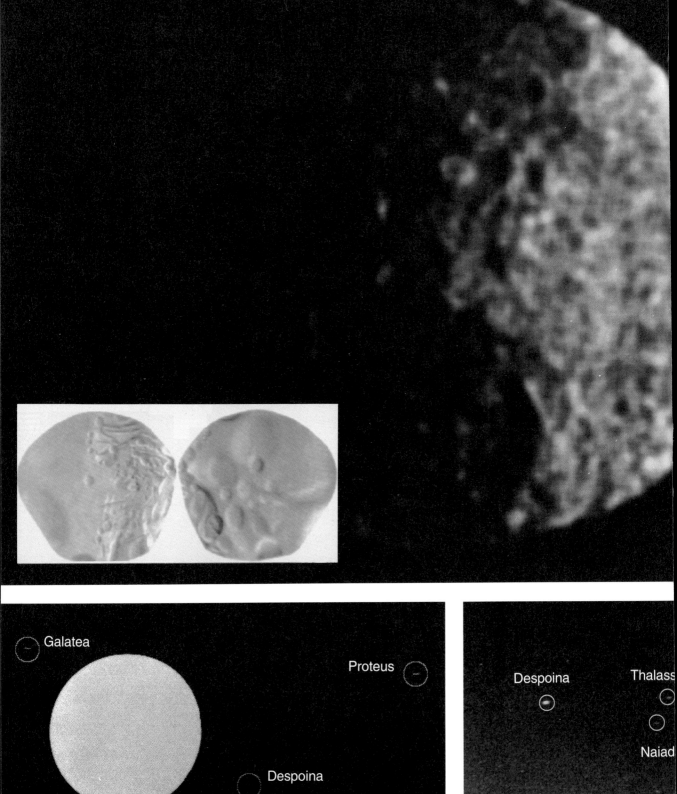

Galatea

Proteus

Despoina

Larissa

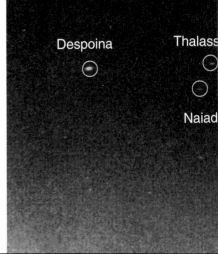

Despoina

Thalass

Naiad

New Moons

In August 1989, *Voyager 2* flew near Neptune and spotted six more satellites circling the planet. These moons are all quite close to Neptune and are estimated to be anywhere from 30 to 260 miles (50 to 420 km) across. They reflect only small amounts of light. Because of their darkness, small size, and great distance from Earth, they are difficult to observe from Earth.

Like all the other known smaller satellites in the Solar System, Neptune's newly discovered moons are lumpy and irregular. Only large celestial bodies have enough gravitational force to form a round shape.

Top: Neptune's second largest known satellite, Proteus, is a gray, cratered ball. Before *Voyager 2* detected Proteus, Nereid was thought to be Neptune's second largest moon. *Inset: Voyager 2* has provided the only detailed glimpse of Proteus. Scientists can use *Voyager*'s pictures to make maps. In this map, Proteus is split in two – the half that leads the way in the moon's orbit around Neptune, and the half that follows.

Bottom: Four of Neptune's six "new" moons from a *Voyager 2* image *(left)*. The remaining two moons *(right)*.

Neptune Has Rings!

From their viewpoint on Earth, astronomers observed that when Neptune moved in front of a star, the star's light dimmed a little just before Neptune covered it. This was a clue to scientists that there might be rings around Neptune. The rings did not seem to be complete, however. They looked more like arcs.

As *Voyager 2* passed Neptune, it revealed there are three complete rings around the planet. They are thin, without much material in them, and clumpy. The clumps hide the stars more than other parts of the rings do. That's why the rings looked like arcs, rather than full rings, from Earth.

! Of rings we sing!

There are four giant planets in the Solar System, and each of them has rings. The rings of Jupiter, Uranus, and Neptune are all thin and faint and made up of dark particles that cannot be seen clearly from Earth. Space probes proved these rings exist. But Saturn has many broad rings made of bright particles, and these can be seen from Earth through binoculars or even a small telescope. The mystery is not why planets have rings, but why Saturn alone has such magnificent rings.

Opposite: The clumps in Neptune's rings are seen in this *Voyager 2* picture.

Below, top: A sketch of Neptune's "ring," as shown in a British letter written in early 1847. Shortly after Neptune's discovery, some astronomers reported a ring around the planet. But in reality, the rings are much too faint to be seen from Earth.

Below, bottom: Long exposures by *Voyager*'s cameras make Neptune look like a bright glare at the center of this picture. The Neptune ring system is clearly visible.

Violent Winds

Just as on Earth, winds of the other planets seem to be powered by the Sun's heat. Saturn is farther from the Sun than Jupiter, so Saturn has less heat and less violent winds than Jupiter. Uranus, farther still, is quite a quiet planet, as *Voyager 2* has shown. Astronomers expected Neptune to be quieter still.

But *Voyager 2* found that the winds of Neptune are surprisingly violent. They move at speeds of over 400 miles (640 km) an hour. Neptune seems almost as active as Jupiter, even though Neptune gets only 1/20 as much energy from the Sun as Jupiter.

Below: Delicate clouds form in the center of what is known as Neptune's Small Dark Spot. Features as small as 12 miles (20 km) across are visible. The Small Dark Spot appears to rotate clockwise – in the opposite direction of what is known as the Great Dark Spot.

Background: In this drawing, Neptune's atmosphere distorts and multiplies the image of the setting Sun. The view is from just above Neptune's Great Dark Spot.

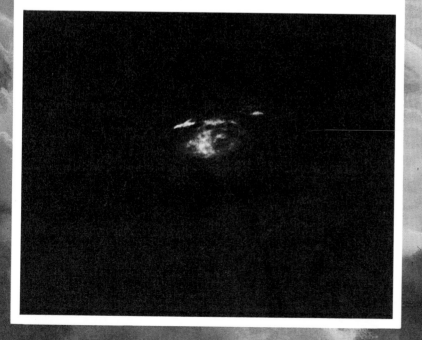

! Neptune –
one far-out planet!

Neptune takes almost 165 years to orbit the Sun, so it has not yet completed a single orbit since its discovery in 1846. It will not come back to the place where it was first seen until 2011. Pluto, which takes 250 years to orbit the Sun, is usually the farthest known planet. But during a twenty-year period in Pluto's orbit, it is a bit closer to the Sun than Neptune is. We are in that period now, so until 1999, Neptune is the farthest planet from the Sun.

© 1989 BENSUSEN

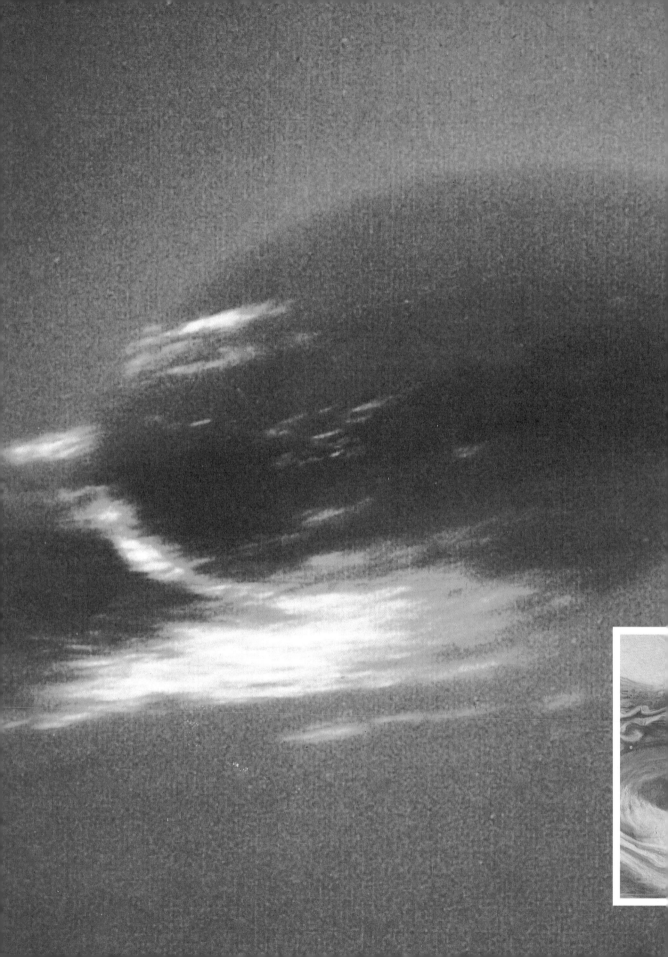

Neptune's Great Surprise

Voyager 2 showed that Neptune is full of surprises. But perhaps *Voyager*'s most astonishing discovery was that Neptune has something in its atmosphere that is much like the Great Red Spot on Jupiter.

Neptune's Great Dark Spot has the same shape as Jupiter's spot. Neptune's spot is deep blue in color, however, with a slight reddish tint. It is smaller than Jupiter's spot, but if Neptune were scaled to match Jupiter in size, the spots would be the same size, too.

Like Jupiter's red spot, Neptune's dark spot seems to be a never-ending giant hurricane. Its width is about the same as Earth's diameter. In *Voyager 2* pictures, scientists saw bright, thin clouds move over the Great Dark Spot. This indicates that the spot is lower in Neptune's atmosphere than its clouds.

Opposite: Neptune's Great Dark Spot, as seen by *Voyager 2* from a distance of 1.7 million miles (2.8 million km). Methane gas streaming over the spot forms the ever-present white clouds. *Inset:* Jupiter's Great Red Spot, seen here in a *Voyager 1* image, is about three times as wide as Earth.

Left: Jupiter is no longer the only planet known to have a giant storm. The Great Red Spot, seen here in Jupiter's Southern Hemisphere, is strikingly similar to Neptune's dark oval.

Planetary Magnetism

Jupiter has a magnetic field that is much stronger than Earth's. Saturn and Uranus have magnetic fields, too. *Voyager 2* has detected a magnetic field around Neptune, as well.

In order to have a magnetic field, a gaseous giant planet must have a liquid region somewhere in its interior that conducts electricity. On the whole, Neptune seems like the other giant planets. It is made up mostly of gaseous substances that get hot and dense in the interior. It may have a small rocky core. But some scientists think the source of Neptune's magnetic field may be closer to its surface than to its core.

Opposite: Neptune's core of rock is surrounded by a gaseous "envelope." The enlarged section shows the cloud layers of Neptune's stormy atmosphere.

Inset: Voyager scientists were surprised to learn how far the axis of Neptune's magnetic field tilts away from the axis of the planet's rotation. The magnetic field also seems to be centered on a spot some distance from Neptune's center. *Voyager 2* showed that Neptune's magnetic field is similar to that of Uranus – and very different from Earth's.

❓ *The case of the tipped magnetic fields*

According to scientists, a celestial body's magnetic field ought to line up with the body's axis of rotation. For some reason, Earth's magnetic field tips a little bit toward its axis. Uranus's magnetic field tips way over. Uranus's axis is turned so the planet seems to be rolling on its side. This might be why its magnetic field is so tilted. But Neptune's axis is much more nearly upright, and yet its magnetic field is greatly tipped, too. Why? Scientists are not sure.

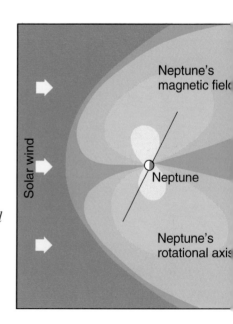

Solar wind

Neptune's magnetic field

Neptune

Neptune's rotational axis

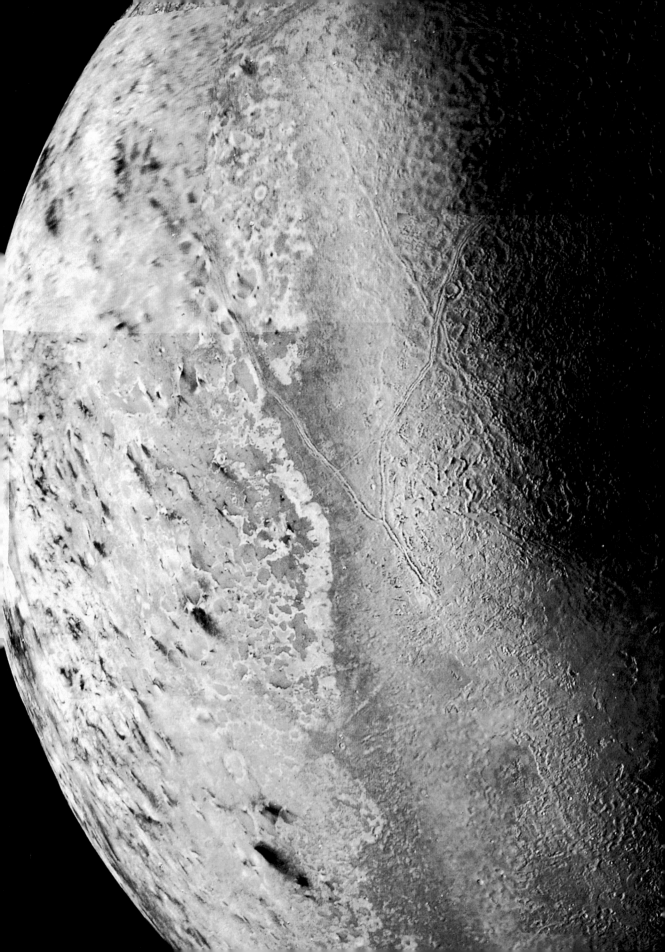

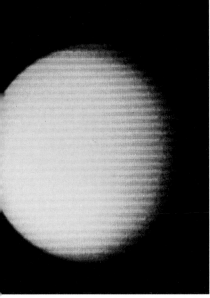

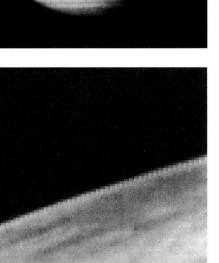

Triton – Neptune's Largest Moon

Voyager 2 has also passed near Triton, Neptune's largest satellite. Triton's diameter is about 1,700 miles (2,740 km), as compared with Earth's Moon's at 2,160 miles (3,480 km) across.

Some scientists expected Triton to be similar to Saturn's large satellite, Titan. Titan is large enough to hold a hazy atmosphere that hides its surface. But the smaller Triton has only a very thin atmosphere, and its surface is clearly visible.

Opposite: Scientists combined a dozen *Voyager 2* photos to make this image of Triton. Methane ice altered by sunlight may create the pink color.

Top: The surface of Titan, Saturn's largest moon, hides beneath a hazy atmosphere of methane and nitrogen.

Center: Triton's thin atmosphere suspends icy particles that form a thin haze around the moon.

Bottom: Circular depressions may be caused by the melting and collapsing of Triton's icy surface.

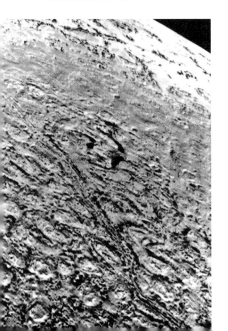

? *Wrong-way Triton – a captured asteroid?*

Most satellites move around their planet in the same direction the planet turns on its axis. Six of the Solar System's seven largest satellites, including Earth's Moon, move in the normal direction, west to east – all except Triton. Neptune rotates west to east as Earth does, but Triton moves around Neptune east to west. Could Triton be an asteroid or a giant comet-like body that was captured by Neptune's gravity long ago? Scientists do not know for sure.

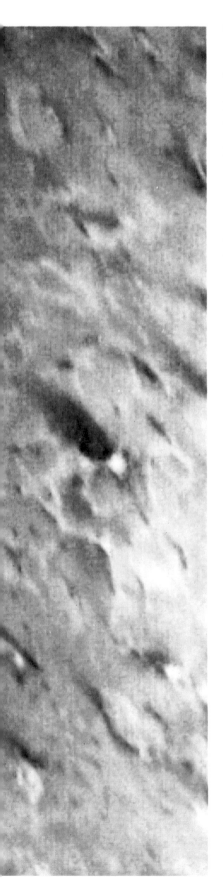

Triton's Ice Volcanoes

Triton's surface is an icy landscape of frozen nitrogen. This frozen surface reflects sunlight well, so Triton is much brighter than the other moons of Neptune. Triton is the coldest Solar System body yet observed at -397° Fahrenheit (-238° Centigrade). Triton's south polar ice cap looks pink. Scientists think some of the color comes from methane ice bombarded for years by high-energy particles.

Nitrogen ice may allow the feeble sunlight to warm deeper layers of Triton's crust. Once warmed, though, these deep layers cannot quickly cool because the nitrogen ice above will not let infrared radiation escape as easily as it lets light in. Scientists think this may be the source of energy for Triton's biggest surprise – ice volcanoes that throw a mixture of nitrogen, methane, and other substances high above the frigid surface.

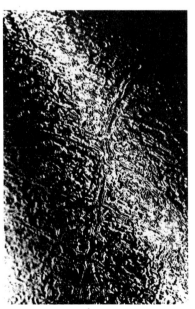

Opposite: An artist imagines ice volcanoes erupting in Triton's thin atmosphere.

Far left: Dark streaks pepper the surface of Triton's south polar cap. They may be the result of material being shot into the atmosphere by ice volcanoes. *Voyager 2* has observed two such eruptions in progress – the plumes of the geysers reaching a height of nearly 5 miles (8 km). The sources of the eruptions are seen as circular white spots in this photo.

Left: Fault lines cut across portions of Triton's surface.

Triton: Captured in the Cosmos?

Triton's odd orbit leads some scientists to think that it formed elsewhere and was later captured by Neptune.

Indeed, astronomers recently discovered dozens of large comet and asteroid-like bodies lying beyond Neptune. Some scientists call them "plutinos" because they may be the kinds of objects from which Pluto formed – and maybe Triton as well.

But Pluto's own moon, Charon, more closely resembles the moons of Saturn than it does Pluto!

Above: Johann Gottfried Galle shared in Neptune's discovery.

Opposite, top: Voyager 2 has provided the best glimpse of Neptune's moon Triton, so far. A single crater, about 8 miles (13 km) wide, can be seen near the center of this view. The large, flat depression around it may be the remains of an older, larger crater filled in by the thick ice lavas that have reshaped Triton's surface. The rough area in the center of the depression may mark a recent eruption.

Opposite, bottom: With the help of computers, scientists can create different perspectives on *Voyager* images. Imagine yourself flying high above Triton, looking toward this depression in its surface.

! *Sometimes two wrongs do make a right!*

When Adams and Leverrier calculated Neptune's position, they did not know how far beyond Uranus it might be. Each incorrectly guessed that Neptune was much farther away than it really is, and much larger than it really is. But these two mistakes canceled each other, and each man ended up predicting that Neptune would be where it actually is.

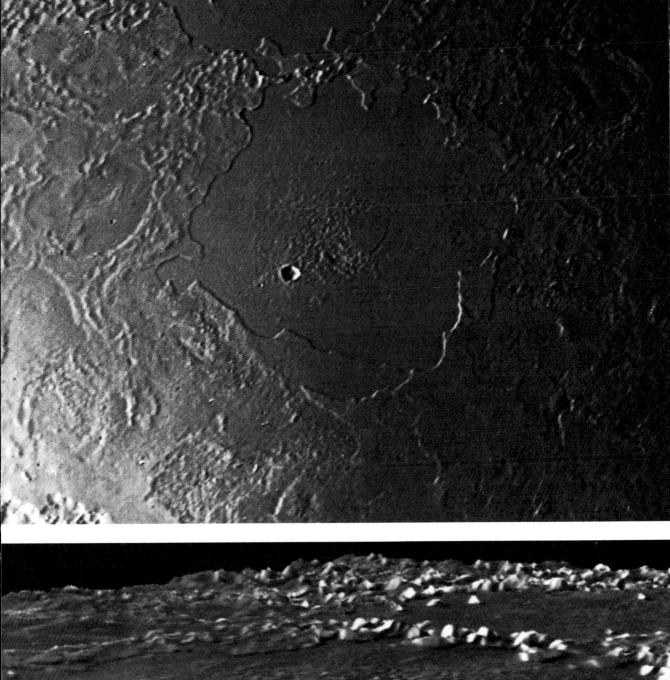
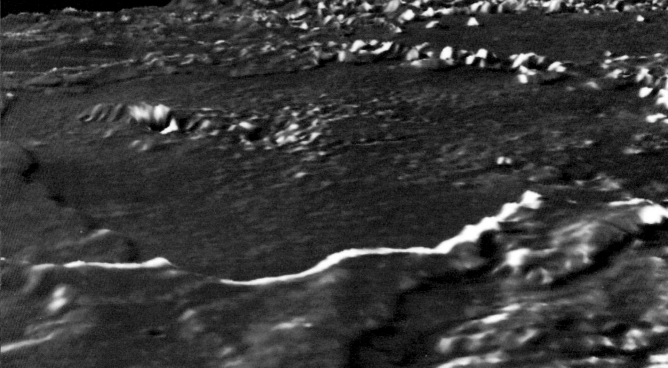

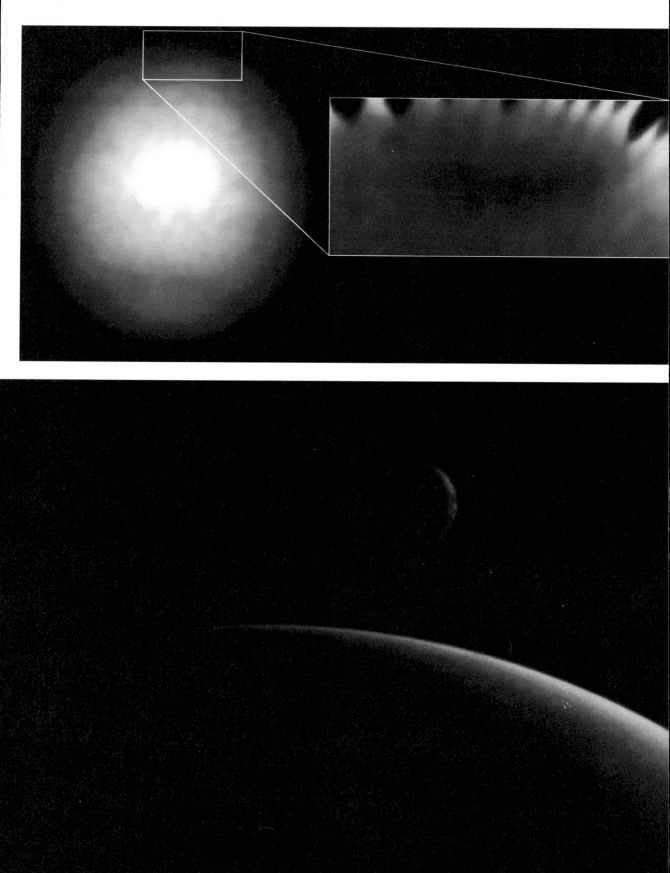

A Journey of Discovery – *Voyager 2*

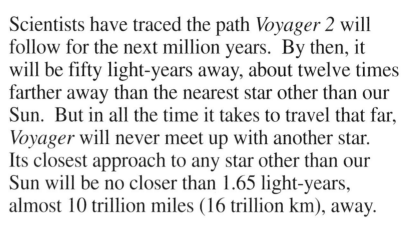

Opposite, top: Scientists studying Neptune with the Hubble Space Telescope in 1994 were surprised to find that the Great Dark Spot seen by *Voyager 2* had disappeared – and that an identical spot had formed in the opposite hemisphere!

Bottom: Voyager 2's farewell photograph of Neptune and Triton, both slender crescents from the spacecraft's viewpoint.

Scientists have traced the path *Voyager 2* will follow for the next million years. By then, it will be fifty light-years away, about twelve times farther away than the nearest star other than our Sun. But in all the time it takes to travel that far, *Voyager* will never meet up with another star. Its closest approach to any star other than our Sun will be no closer than 1.65 light-years, almost 10 trillion miles (16 trillion km), away.

Scientists do not know what surprises await *Voyager* as it sails through the cosmos. But for now, Neptune holds the prize for the most news beamed back home by our faithful robot.

Until we can send spacecraft to Neptune again, the Hubble Space Telescope will supply scientists with additional data. Hubble can see features in Neptune's cloud tops that are 620 miles (1,000 km) across – and it has already served up a puzzle for planetary scientists! When *Voyager 2* passed Neptune in 1989, its cameras revealed the Great Dark Spot in the planet's Southern Hemisphere. Yet Hubble images taken in late 1994 indicate that the Great Dark Spot had vanished – and that a new dark spot now occupies Neptune's Northern Hemisphere. Scientists do not quite understand what's going on in Neptune's atmosphere!

Fact File: A Distant Giant

Neptune is our Solar System's fourth largest known planet. It is also the eighth farthest from the Sun. Only tiny Pluto has an orbit that stretches farther from the Sun than Neptune's. In fact, Neptune is so far from the Sun that its "year" equals nearly 165 Earth years. For about twenty of those years, Pluto's unusual orbit takes it within Neptune's orbit. This means that Neptune is then farther from the Sun than Pluto.

With the journey of *Voyager 2* past Neptune in 1989, and with recent observations made by the Hubble Space Telescope, many mysteries about this cold and beautiful planet were cleared up, and many previously unknown secrets were revealed.

Stay tuned for more as scientists continue their studies of the magnificent, distant giant – Neptune.

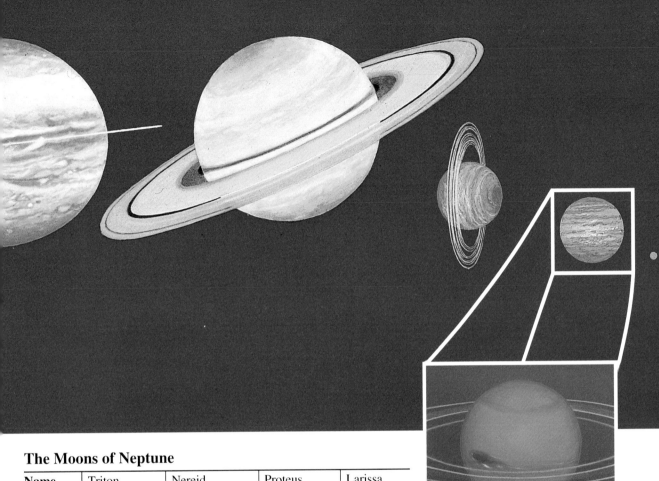

The Moons of Neptune

Name	Triton	Nereid	Proteus	Larissa
Diameter	1,700 miles (2,740 km)	210 miles (340 km)	260 miles (420 km)	120 miles (190 km)
Distance from Neptune	220,300 miles (354,460 km)	3,424,000 miles (5,509,700 km)	73,000 miles (117,600 km)	45,700 miles (73,600 km)

Name	Despoina	Galatea	Thalassa	Naiad
Diameter	90 miles (145 km)	100 miles (160 km)	55 miles (90 km)	30 miles (50 km)
Distance from Neptune	32,600 miles (52,500 km)	38,500 miles (62,000 km)	31,000 miles (50,000 km)	30,000 miles (48,200 km)

Top: The Sun and its Solar System family, *left to right:* Mercury, Venus, Earth, Mars, Jupiter, Saturn, Uranus, Neptune, and Pluto.

Inset: Neptune and its moons.

Neptune: How It Measures Up to Earth

Planet	Diameter	Rotation Period	Period of Orbit around Sun (length of year)	Known Moons	Surface Gravity
Neptune	30,450 miles (49,000 km)	17 hours, 42 minutes	164 years, 288 days	8	1.13*
Earth	7,925 miles (12,753 km)	23 hours, 56 minutes	365.25 days	1	1.00*

*Multiply your weight by this number to find out how much you would weigh on this planet.

Planet	Distance from Sun (nearest-farthest)	Least Time It Takes for Light to Travel to Earth
Neptune	2.7-2.8 billion miles (4.3-4.5 billion km)	3 hours, 53 minutes
Earth	92-95 million miles (148-153 million km)	—

More Books about Neptune

Astronomy Today: Planets, Stars, Space Exploration. Moche (Random House)
Modern Astronomy. Asimov (Gareth Stevens)
Our Planetary System. Asimov (Gareth Stevens)
The Planets. Barrett (Franklin Watts)
The Planets. Couper (Franklin Watts)
The Planets: Exploring the Solar System. Gallant (Four Winds/Macmillan)

Videos

Neptune: The Farthest Giant. (Gareth Stevens)
Our Solar System. (Gareth Stevens)

Places to Visit

You can explore Neptune and other places in the Universe without leaving Earth.
Here are some museums and centers where you can find a variety of space exhibits.

NASA Lyndon B. Johnson Space Center
2101 NASA Road One
Houston, TX 77058

Australian Museum
6-8 College Street
Sydney, NSW 2000 Australia

International Women's Air and Space Museum
1 Chamber Plaza
Dayton, OH 45402

Edmonton Space and Science Centre
11211 – 142nd Street
Edmonton, Alberta T5M 4A1

National Air and Space Museum
Smithsonian Institution
Seventh and Independence Avenue SW
Washington, D.C. 20560

The Space and Rocket Center
  and Space Camp
One Tranquility Base
Huntsville, AL 35807

Places to Write

Here are some places you can write for more information about Neptune and the other planets.
Be sure to state what kind of information you would like. Include your full name and address
for a reply.

National Space Society
922 Pennsylvania Avenue SE
Washington, D.C. 20003

Sydney Observatory
P. O. Box K346
Haymarket 2000 Australia

Jet Propulsion Laboratory
Teacher Resource Center
4800 Oak Grove Drive
Pasadena, CA 91109

Canadian Space Agency
Communications Department
6767 Route de L'Aeroport
Saint Hubert, Quebec J3Y 8Y9

Glossary

atmosphere: the gases that surround a planet, star, or moon.

axis: the imaginary straight line around which a planet, star, or moon turns.

billion: the number represented by 1 followed by nine zeroes – 1,000,000,000. In some countries, this number is called "a thousand million." In these countries, one billion would then be represented by 1 followed by twelve zeroes – 1,000,000,000,000 – a million million.

diameter: the length of a straight line through the exact center of a circle or sphere. Neptune has a diameter of about 30,450 miles (49,000 km).

giant planets: Jupiter, Saturn, Uranus, and Neptune – the four largest known planets in our Solar System. Also called the gas giants, these planets are made up mostly of gases and lie beyond the asteroid belt that encircles the four inner rocky planets, Mercury, Venus, Mars, and Earth.

gravity: the force that causes astronomical bodies to be drawn to one another and that holds them in their orbits.

Great Dark Spot: a large storm in Neptune's atmosphere, similar to Jupiter's Great Red Spot.

light-year: the distance that light travels in one year — nearly 6 trillion miles (9.6 trillion km).

magnetic field: the force that surrounds a planet like an "atmosphere" of energy.

methane: a colorless, odorless, flammable gas.

Neptune: the ancient Roman god of the sea (called Poseidon by the ancient Greeks). The planet Neptune is named for him because of its sea-like, bluish green color.

rings: thin bands of rock, ice, and dust that circle all the gas giants. Of the four giant planets, Saturn has the most clearly visible rings. They are visible from Earth with a pair of binoculars or a telescope.

rotation: the turning around a central point on an axis.

satellite: a smaller body that orbits a larger body. The Moon is Earth's natural satellite. *Sputnik 1* was Earth's first artificial satellite.

solar wind: tiny particles that travel from the Sun's surface at a speed of 300 miles (480 km) a second.

Voyager 2: the space probe that journeyed past Neptune in 1989, beaming back to Earth pictures and data about Neptune and its moons.

Index

Born in 1920, Isaac Asimov came to the United States as a young boy from his native Russia. As a young man, he was a student of biochemistry. In time, he became one of the most productive writers the world has ever known. His books cover a spectrum of topics, including science, history, language theory, fantasy, and science fiction. His brilliant imagination gained him the respect and admiration of adults and children alike. Sadly, Isaac Asimov died shortly after the publication of the first edition of *Isaac Asimov's Library of the Universe.*

The publishers wish to thank the following for permission to reproduce copyright material: front cover, © Bob Eggleton 1990; 4, Jet Propulsion Laboratory; 5 (both), Yerkes Observatory; 6-7 (upper), Sharon Burris/© Gareth Stevens, Inc.; 6-7 (lower), NASA; 7, Jet Propulsion Laboratory; 8, Sharon Burris/© Gareth Stevens, Inc.; 9 (large), Yerkes Observatory; 9 (inset), Jet Propulsion Laboratory; 10 (upper), Courtesy P. J. Stooke, University of Western Ontario; 10 (lower), 10-11 (upper), 10-11 (lower), Jet Propulsion Laboratory; 12-13 (upper), Collection of Richard Baum; 12-13 (lower), 13, 14, Jet Propulsion Laboratory; 14-15, © Sally Bensusen 1989; 16-17 (large), Jet Propulsion Laboratory; 16-17 (inset), 17, NASA; 18-19, Sharon Burris/© Gareth Stevens, Inc.; 19, © Paul Dimare 1989; 20, 21 (all), Jet Propulsion Laboratory; 22, © Paul Dimare 1989; 23 (both), Jet Propulsion Laboratory; 24, Yerkes Observatory; 25 (both), Jet Propulsion Laboratory; 26, H. Hammel (Massachusetts Institute of Technology) and NASA; 26-27, Jet Propulsion Laboratory; 28-29, © Sally Bensusen; 29 (inset), © Thomas O. Miller/Studio "X," 1990.